MARY - LOW SCHENCK

SO-AXR-163

The Magic Flute

THE MAGIC FLUTE

An Opera in two acts

Music by W. A. MOZART

English version after the Libretto

of Schikaneder and Giesecke

by W. H. AUDEN

and CHESTER KALLMAN

Random House   New York

FIRST PRINTING

© Copyright, 1955, as an unpublished work, by W. H. Auden and Chester Kallman. © Copyright, 1956, by W. H. Auden and Chester Kallman. All rights, including the rights of reproduction in whole or in part, are reserved under International and Pan-American Copyright Conventions. Published in New York by
Random House, Inc., and simultaneously in Toronto, Canada, by Random House
of Canada, Limited.

Caution: Professionals and amateurs are hereby warned that *The Magic Flute*,
being fully protected under the copyright laws of the United States, the British
Empire, including the Dominion of Canada, and all other countries of the Copyright Union, is subject to royalty. All rights, including professional, amateur,
motion picture, recitation, lecturing, public reading, radio and television broadcasting, and the rights of translation into foreign languages, are reserved. Any
reproduction or performance of this work in whole or in part is an infringement
of copyright and is prohibited unless expressly authorized in writing by the
Authors. Particular emphasis is laid on the question of readings, permission for
which must be obtained in writing from the Authors. All inquiries should be
addressed to Curtis Brown, Limited, 347 Madison Avenue, New York 17, N. Y.

Library of Congress Catalog Card Number: 56–8794
Manufactured in the United States of America by H. Wolff, New York

Illustrations by Rouben Ter-Arutunian

DESIGN: Marshall Lee

To ANNE *and* IRVING WEISS
This Tale where true loves meet and mate, Brute, Brave,
Grave, Laughter-loving, Great,
Wee, Wise and Dotty translate
To Music, we dedicate.

PREFACE

Probably no other opera calls more for translation than *Die Zauberflöte,* and for a translation that is also an interpretation. This does not demand nor excuse transporting the action to that hospitable and mythical Dixie which has had to put up with guests as unlikely as *Carmen, Aïda* and *The Cherry Orchard. Die Zauberflöte* must remain in its own Never-Never Land, but that land itself cries out for sharper definition.

Even the most ardent opera fans, who can easily take such absurdities as the plot of *I Puritani,* are apt to find the libretto of *Die Zauberflöte* hard to swallow, and with some justification; though they may not always be certain what it is that upsets them. So long as an opera libretto is just that and no more, we ask of it only that it provide lyrical characters and lyrical situations; but if, whether by accident or design, it should have a significance in itself, apart from anything the composer may do with it, then any muddle or contradictions in the story cannot be covered up by the music, even music by Mozart.

It is highly dangerous for a librettist, unless he knows exactly what he is doing, which Schikaneder and Giesecke certainly did not, to make use of fairy-story material, for such material almost always expresses universal and profound human experiences which will make a fool of anyone who ignores or trivializes them. Yet its very confusions, perhaps, give this libretto a fascination it might lack had the librettists stuck to what was, ostensibly, their original intention: to write a straight fairy-tale about the rescue of a young girl from a wicked sorcerer.

If their libretto also seems peculiarly silly, it is because a proper treatment of its material would have made it one of the greatest libretti ever written. It is not surprising that, even as it stands, it inspired Goethe to write a sequel (though not, it must be confessed, a very good one).

It is rare for the story of a successful opera to be interesting in itself. Even Don Juan, a character of profound extra-musical significance, cannot be said to have a story since, by definition, he cannot or will not change himself; he can only be shown as triumphant and invulnerable (the Duke in *Rigoletto*), or in his fall (*Don Giovanni*). He cannot be shown as both in the same opera, for the transition from triumph to ruin depends not on him but on the will of Heaven. The characters in *Die Zauberflöte*, on the other hand, have a real history in which what happens next always depends upon what they choose now.

To discover what, if anything, can be done to improve the libretto, one must begin by trying to detect the basic elements of the story. This story combines two themes, both of great interest. The first and most basic of these is the story of a change in relation between the Dionysian principle and the

Apollonian, Night and Day, the instinctive and the rational, the unconscious and the conscious, here symbolized as female and male, respectively.

What has been a relationship of antagonism, the war between the Queen and Sarastro, is finally replaced by a relationship of mutual affection and reconciliation, the marriage of Pamina and Tamino. (Who Pamina's father was, we are never told; we only learn that he was the maker of the flute.) Though the conscious and rational must take the responsibility for the instinctive, and hence be the "superior" partner, neither can exist without the other. What the libretto fails to make clear is that, though the Queen must be defeated in order that the New Age may come, her defeat completes Sarastro's task: he must now hand on the crown to Tamino and pass away like Prospero in *The Tempest.* The Freemasonry of the authors may be partly responsible for their vagueness on this point, but what is most surprising is that they should have allowed the Queen to play such a positive part: she saves Tamino's life, she shows him Pamina's portrait and even gives him the magic flute without which he could never have gotten through the trials successfully. Again, whether by sheer luck or by sound instinct, the librettists showed the Messengers of the Gods, the three Boy Spirits, as equally at home in the Queen's realm and in Sarastro's. This is surprising, because to allow the Night a creative role is very untypical of the Enlightenment doctrines for which they stood and, had they denied it to the Queen, they would have spared themselves the most obvious criticism which is always brought against them, namely, that without any warning the audience has to switch its sympathies at the end of the First Act.

Their other defect in the handling of this theme is one of taste rather than understanding: a perfectly proper symbolization of the two opposing Principles as male and female gave them an opportunity—which, alas, they could not resist —to make cheap vaudeville jokes about women.

The second theme is an educational one: how does a person discover his vocation and what does the discovery entail? When the opera opens, Tamino has been wandering about the desert without aim or direction, driven by some vague dissatisfaction, and is therefore, like all adolescents, in danger from forces in the depth of his nature which he cannot understand or control (the serpent). Saved from this, he is shown Pamina's picture and falls in love with her, i.e., he believes that he has discovered his future vocation, but only time will show if his belief is genuine or fantastic; he has, as yet, no notion of what this vocation will involve.

That is what Sarastro has to teach him, namely, that any vocation demands faith, patience and courage. For each of these, then, he has to be tested: he must endure the false doubts of the Queen's three Ladies, the pain of making Pamina suffer through his silence, and, finally, the terrors of Fire and Water.

Pamina, the representative of the emotions, has also to learn through suffering to endure the unwelcome attentions of Monostatos, Tamino's incomprehensible silence, her mother's curse and, finally, together with her lover, the trial by Fire and Water; for emotion has to learn that there are other values besides its own.

In Act Two, as written, Pamina's troubles with Monostatos and the Queen precede the trial of Tamino's silence and departure. We have reversed this order for the following reasons. It does not seem natural that, having seen her fall into Tamino's arms at the end of Act One, she should appear, when we see her next, to have forgotten his existence. Secondly, the effect of Monostatos and her mother upon her would be a much greater temptation to suicidal despair if she had to endure them after she imagines her lover has deserted her rather than before, when she could console herself with the thought of him and even call on him for help and guidance. Thirdly, we wished to make her appearance in the Finale with a dagger more plausible and more dramatic.

In the original libretto, the Queen gives her this dagger, Monostatos takes it away from her, a long interval elapses during which we have forgotten all about the instrument, and then, suddenly, there she is with it again. How did she get it back?

Here is the order of the numbers in Act Two as arranged by us, with the original order in figures on the right.

Aria and Chorus: *O Isis und Osiris.*	1
Duet: *Bewahret euch.*	2
Quintet: *Wie, wie, wie.*	3
Trio: *Seid uns zum zweiten Mal.*	7
Aria: *Ach, ich fühl's.*	8
Trio: *Soll ich dich, Teurer.*	10

Naturally, a change in order involves a change in key relationships. Were the music continuous, this would probably be a fatal objection, but it is not. If there are ears which can carry through each passage of spoken dialogue a memory of the last chord before it began, while anxiously anticipating the first chord after it has ended, they are more sensitive and less attentive than ours.

Over against Tamino, the Quest Hero, who has to *become* authentic, stands Papageno, the uncorrupted child of Nature, for whom authenticity means accepting the fact that he *is* what he is. Quite properly, his hut lies in the Queen's realm, not Sarastro's. He successfully passes his trial and is rewarded with his mirror image, Papagena; but this is so casually treated in the original libretto that the audience does not always notice what the trial is. Asked if he is prepared to endure the trials by Fire and Water like his master, he says No, they are not for the likes of him. Threatened then by the Priest that if he refuses he will never win Papagena, he replies, ". . . In that case, I'll remain single." It is by this last answer that his humility is revealed, and for which he receives his reward.

This clear division between the Hero who must be brave enough to dare and the Hero who must be humble enough to stay home is smudged in the original due to the actor's vanity of Schikaneder, who wanted to be on stage and get laughs as much as possible.

For example, it is absurd and embarrassing to have Papageno present and being "funny" during the pathetic scene *Ach, ich fühl's*. Also, Tamino can take vows because for him they have meaning, and for the audience they have the dramatic excitement of causing it to wonder whether he will keep them. But a child of Nature cannot take vows because they apply to the future, and he exists in a continuous present; there is no interest in hearing Papageno take a vow of silence which we know perfectly well in advance he will not keep because the notion of a vow is incomprehensible to him.

The only trial, therefore, that we have allowed him to share with Tamino is that of being frightened by the three Ladies in the *Wie, wie, wie* Quintet, from which, anyway, he cannot, for musical reasons, be absent. This fright, then, confirms his decision not to accompany Tamino; he is officially excused from doing so, and the two say good-bye to each other. As we now have it, it is only after he has left, and shortly before Pamina's entrance, that the vow of silence is imposed upon Tamino.

There is historical evidence that Mozart found Schikaneder's horseplay in the role of Papageno excessive and irritating (there is practically none in the musical sections), yet the horseplay has remained "traditional." And it may be that audiences, vexed by a lack of any clear narrative thread, have seized upon this one consistent wrong note and helped, by their overdelighted reactions, to keep this tradition alive.

Papageno must be comic, but he should not be low farce. A Noble Savage, he enjoys a happiness and self-assurance which Tamino, and even Sarastro, cannot share; one might even say that he is the unlettered aristocrat, they but learned clerks. This presents the translator with a stylistic problem. Fortunately, pastoral, a literary genre created by Theocritus and Virgil for just such characters, with its paradox of humble concerns and sophisticated diction, has been popular in English literature since the sixteenth century; in Germany, there are few examples, and even these are an imitation of French models rather than an indigenous product.

Opposed to Papageno, the uncorrupted child of Nature, stands Monostatos, his corrupted twin. Like Papageno, he is incapable of enduring the trials; unlike the former, however, he lacks the humility that would accept a variety of Papagena. No, he demands the heroine, Pamina. He is clearly another version of Caliban.

We have written the dialogue in verse, because it seemed to us the right medium for the spoken word in an *opera magica;* it obliterates any trace of *verismo,* and it keeps the comic passages within decent bounds.

Translation is a dubious business at best and we are inclined to agree with those who believe that operas should always be given in their native tongue. However, if audiences demand them in their own, they must accept the consequences. Obviously, the texture and weight of the original words set by the composer are an element in his orchestration and any change of the words is therefore an alteration of the music itself. Yet the goal of the translator, however unattainable, must be to make audiences believe that the words they are hearing are the words which the composer actually set, which means that a too-literal translation of the original text may sometimes prove a falsification.

Assuming that he is a competent versifier and can read a score, the translator can copy the original prosody and rhyme schemes and know that his version will fit the notes, but it does not necessarily follow that he should be content with this. In doing an aria, for example, it is often better, once he has grasped its emotional mood and general tenor, to put the actual words out of his mind and concentrate upon writing as good an English lyric as possible. His real headaches, of course, begin when he comes to nonlyrical connecting passages where the meaning of what is being sung has an informative or dramaturgical importance. Some of the stumbling blocks we encountered in translating this opera we have described in the end-notes.

We have every sympathy for those who are distressed by the slightest deviation from a score they know so well and have loved for so long, just as a British ear is jarred every time Americans pray "Our Father *who* art in heaven" instead of the "Our Father *which*" it has heard since childhood, but if they wish to enjoy the advantages of opera in English, they must put up with the drawbacks.

W. H. A.

C. K.

Dramatis Personae

SARASTRO, *a High Priest*

TAMINO, *a Prince*

PAPAGENO, *a bird-catcher*

MONOSTATOS, *servant to Sarastro*

FIRST PRIEST

SECOND PRIEST

TWO MEN IN ARMOR

THREE SLAVES

ASTRAFIAMMANTE, *Queen of the Night*

PAMINA, *her daughter*

PAPAGENA

THREE LADIES, *attendants on the Queen*

THREE SPIRITS

CHORUS

The Magic Flute was commissioned by the National Broadcasting Company and produced on television by the NBC Opera Theatre on Sunday, January 15, 1956, with the following cast and production staff:

TAMINO, William Lewis
Attendants on the Queen of the Night:
    FIRST ATTENDANT, Françoise Martinet
    Her Voice, Frances Paige
    SECOND ATTENDANT, Barbara Milberg
    Her Voice, Joan Moynagh
    THIRD ATTENDANT, Eda Lioy
    Her Voice, Helen Vanni
PAPAGENO, John Reardon
ASTRAFIAMMANTE, *Queen of the Night,* Laurel Hurley
FIRST SPIRIT, Tommy Burke
His Voice, Betty Wilson
SECOND SPIRIT, Phil Neuheller
His Voice, Russell Oberlin
THIRD SPIRIT, Dow Thompson
His Voice, Charles Bressler
FIRST SLAVE, David Shapiro
SECOND SLAVE, Billy Rollo
THIRD SLAVE, Harry Davis
MONOSTATOS, Andrew McKinley
PAMINA, Leontyne Price
FIRST PRIEST, Chester Watson
SARASTRO, Yi-Kwei Sze
SECOND PRIEST, Norman Rose

THIRD PRIEST, Alfred Shirley

PAPAGENA, Adelaide Bishop

FIRST ARMORED MAN, Walter Carlih

His Voice, Richard Cassilly

SECOND ARMORED MAN, John Vivyan

His Voice, Chester Watson

STAFF FOR PRODUCTION

Scenery and Costumes designed by Rouben Ter-Arutunian

English Translation by W. H. Auden and Chester Kallman

Special Production Consultant, Lincoln Kirstein

Stage Director, George Balanchine

Associate Producer, Charles Polacheck

Director, Kirk Browning

Music and Artistic Director, Peter Herman Adler

Producer, Samuel Chotzinoff

Proem

Queen Astrafiammante, she
  Long ruled the primal Night,
In realms of dream had reigned supreme,
  Until there came the Light.

But she defied that civil guide,
  Refused to share her throne,
With the High Gods became at odds
  And fled to dwell alone,

Deep underground a refuge found,
  Hating all love and joy,
And, plotting there in her despair
  Sarastro to destroy,

That high priest good whose Brotherhood
  Adored the rising Sun,
With female wile she did beguile
  Among his Order one.

A daughter she bore to her paramour,
  Pamina was her name,
Gentle and fair beyond compare
  Despite her birth in shame.

Commanded by the Gods on high
  This maiden to instruct,
Sarastro then from her mother's den
  Pamina did abduct.

Predestined she, as you will see,
  To serve the High Gods' plan,
That through this child might be reconciled
  The Dark and Light in Man.

Requiring too a bridegroom who
  Their purpose shall effect,
A noble youth in love with truth,
  Tamino, they select.

Beginning now, our play shows how
  What the High Gods intend
Through peril and doubt is brought about
  That all things well may end.

ACT ONE

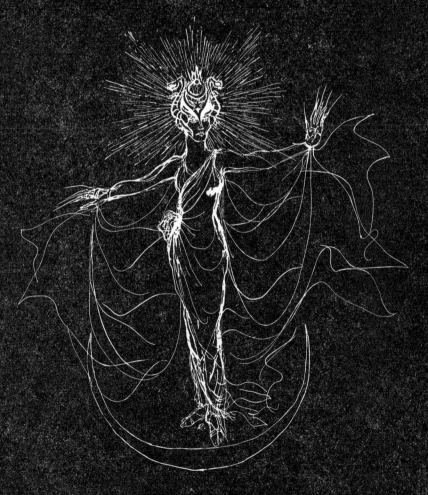

Astrafiammante

Scene I

[*A rocky desert. In the background a great cliff. Enter* TAMINO *in the last stages of exhaustion and terror.*]

TAMINO

O save me, have mercy, ye gods, or I perish!
Have mercy and save me, ye Heavenly Powers!
A venomous serpent pursues me with jaws open wide to devour me!
    [*Serpent appears.*]
With glittering eye he slowly draws nigh.
Ah, pitiless! Am I to die in agony?
Have mercy, mercy, save me, save . . . [*Falls.*] I die!
    [*Faints.*]
      [*Enter the* THREE LADIES *of* The Queen *carrying silver javelins with which they slay the serpent.*]

TRIO

LADIES

Die, monster, die! Pernicious bane!
'Tis done, 'tis done, the deed is done,
The serpent slain.

From terror free and mortal harm,
The hero lies, saved by a woman's arm.
> [*They inspect the unconscious* TAMINO.]

1ST LADY
What grace of feature, how manly a mien!

2ND LADY
Such noble beauty I have never seen.

3RD LADY
So fair a form . . . to paint, I mean.

LADIES
Should I submit to bonds of love,
How soon would he my captor prove.
Now to the palace haste we all, then,
To tell the Queen what has befallen;
Perhaps this handsome youth can cure
Her burning grief, her joy restore.

1ST LADY
You bring the Queen our news;
I ought to stay with him.

2ND LADY
You two go, if you choose;
I want to stay with him.

3RD LADY
Excuse me, I refuse;
I mean to stay with him.

LADIES
> [*aside*]
I see their plan!
Do they believe they can deceive me so?

They want to be alone, I know,
Alone with him, I know, I know:
No, no, that shan't be so.

How sweet with him all day to dally
Alone in some secluded valley;
The thought brings rapture to my heart.
It cannot be: 'tis best we part.
The pleasing vision is in vain.
Fair youth, farewell; our idylls end:
Farewell; I stay your unknown friend
Until we meet again.
Your friend I shall remain,
Though moons may wax and wane,
In pleasure or in pain,
In sunshine or in rain.

———————

[*Exeunt* LADIES.]

TAMINO
[*coming to*]
How is it possible? Before my eyes,
Stretched out in death, the dreadful serpent lies,
And here I stand alive, preserved by Fate,
But for what purpose? How long must I wait
A vision of the future She intends?
[*The sound of pan-pipes approaching.*]
What uncouth shepherd now the path descends?
[*He hides. Enter* PAPAGENO.]

S O N Gᵃ

PAPAGENO

The lark, the ruddock and the willow-wren
And the jolly nightingale I ken;
In vain do all the pretty little creatures fly
When they the tall bird-catcher spy.
With a whistle I their ears decoy
And many a cunning snare employ,
So that I can merry merry-hearted be,
For all the birds belong to me.

For the snipe, the partridge, cock and hen,
The melodious mavis, too, I ken;
In vain do all the pretty little creatures fly
When they the tall bird-catcher spy.
Had I a maiden-catching net,
Fair maids by dozens I should daily get;
Had I a cage to keep them in,
I would lock it with a golden pin.

If all the pretty girls on earth were mine,
On spice and sugar they should dine,
And she that was the prettiest
Should get more sugar than the rest.
How sweetly would we bill and coo
As married turtledoves may freely do:
When at night she laid herself beside me, I
Would rock her with a lullaby.

TAMINO
[*coming out*]
Good friend!

PAPAGENO
[*startled*]
Who's there?

TAMINO
Stop! Do not run away,
But help a stranger who has lost his way.

PAPAGENO
A stranger here is a lost stranger since
There *are* no strangers here. Who are you, pray?

TAMINO
Tamino is my name, my title Prince.

PAPAGENO
[*bowing*]
This man is Papageno, known as Me,
Bird-catcher to Her Glorious Majesty
Queen Astrafiammante, She who reigns
Unseen. What brings a prince to her domains?

TAMINO
Dream voices that I could not understand
Called me and bade me leave my native land:
By perilous and solitary ways,
Through forest, fen and desert many days
My feet have wandered with uncertain aim,
Driven by longings which I cannot name,
Seeking I know not what. Today it seemed
The grave must be the quest of which I dreamed,
But I was rescued by some giant's hand.

PAPAGENO

What giant? There are no giants in this land.

TAMINO

What man could such a mighty deed have done?
Is this a land of heroes?

PAPAGENO

There are none;
This is a realm of women, but for me.

TAMINO

[*embracing* PAPAGENO]

Then . . . then . . . it must be . . . [*Aside*] But how can
it be?

[*to* PAPAGENO]

Dear friend, my friend forever, it was you
That saved my life and this great serpent slew.

PAPAGENO

Where? [*Sees corpse.*] Help! [*Tries to run.* TAMINO *holds
him.*]

TAMINO

Your hand!

PAPAGENO

It's quite dead?

TAMINO

You should know
That slew it. The knightly modesty you show
Is equal to your valor. Tell me how,
Swordless, you did it.

PAPAGENO

[*aside*]

What shall I say now?

[*to* TAMINO]
O, it's quite simple once you know the way;
I've slain far bigger serpents in my day.
  [*The* THREE LADIES *appear and advance with threatening
    looks.*]

LADIES
Papageno!

PAPAGENO
          Ah,
Here come my friends with bread and figs and wine
To pay me for these pretty birds of mine.

TAMINO
[*aside*]
To me they neither look nor sound like friends!

LADIES
Papageno!

PAPAGENO
Ladies, good day! The Queen was pleased, I trust,
With the white owl I sent her.

1ST LADY
                    The Queen is just,
And to her servant, Papageno, sends . . .

PAPAGENO
[*aside*]
What have I done? I do not like her tone.

1ST LADY
Not wine, but water,

PAPAGENO
          Oh!

2ND LADY

Not bread, but stone.

3RD LADY

No figs . . .

PAPAGENO

O! gentle lady! No! No!

3RD LADY

[*putting a padlock on his mouth*]

. . . but

This padlock . . .

PAPAGENO

Hm!

3RD LADY

. . . his lying mouth to shut.

LADIES

So shall all be punished who
Boast of deeds they did not do.

[*Exit* PAPAGENO.]

3RD LADY

'Twas we who saved you, Prince: enough of that.
Your coming known, the Queen is pleased thereat:
Whereof in token now she sends you this,

[*Hands* TAMINO *a miniature.*]

The dearest of her treasures, for it is
The portrait of Pamina, her adored
And only daughter. May this face reward
The act of your beholding, your desire
Find its true image. We will now retire.

[*Exeunt* LADIES.]

A R I A

TAMINO
True image of enchanting grace!
O rare perfection's dwelling-place
Where beauty is with virtue shown
More noble than itself alone.

Is she the dream to which I waken,
The pursuit where I am overtaken,
Body and mind and heart and soul?
She is! To love her is my goal.

How do I speak as though I knew her,
When I must find her first and woo her?
O tell me, image, grant a sign—
      Am I her choice?

She will be won—O sweet occasion!—
By gentle force and warm persuasion,
And with her love will answer mine.

———————

I know she is, but that is all I know.
Where is the palace? Thither will I go
To ask the Queen what I must do to find
Her who engages heart and soul and mind.
      [*Thunder.*]

LADIES
[*off-stage*]
She comes! Fire in her eyes, with sceptered hand
The dark instinctive powers to command.
She comes! She comes! Invincible her might!
Hail, Astrafiammante, hail, great Queen of Night!
    [*Lightning. The cliff splits open, revealing* ASTRAFIAM-
    MANTE.]

RECITATIVE
AND ARIA

ASTRAFIAMMANTE
Brave Prince, approach: we welcome you.
We know you gentle, courteous, true,
A young knight born for deeds of love and glory;
My son, hear now a mother's doleful story.

Forlorn, despairing, broken-hearted,
I mourn a daughter night and day;
By evil fate our lives were parted:
A murderer, a heartless fiend stole her away.
O day dark with horror,
Dismay, despair and terror!
I see it still before my eyes,
I hear her loud heart-rending cries.
The thief ignored all supplication—
O help! O help!
She cried and cried again:

But vain her pitiful rogation,
My protestation all in vain,
My frantic weeping all in vain.

You, you, you
Are the hero, her predestined saviour!
Forth, to my daughter's rescue ride!
To the victorious hero I will give her,
And you shall take her for your bride.

[*The cliff closes again.*]

TAMINO
[*dazed*]
Vision of awe and wonder! Who will guide
The eager bridegroom to the promised bride?
[*Enter* PAPAGENO.]

QUINTET

PAPAGENO
Hm, hm, hm, hm, etc.

TAMINO
His wits, by lack of words unwitty,
    Express what he is sentenced to:
By words I can express my pity,
    But that is all my words can do.
[*Enter the* THREE LADIES.]

1ST LADY
[*removes the padlock*]
Our gracious Queen declares through me
She pardons you and sets you free.

PAPAGENO
Good Papageno's tongue can wag now.

2ND LADY
Remember, do not lie or brag now!

PAPAGENO
The truth is wiser, I agree.

ALL
Let this to all false tongues a warning be.

So shall the Truth all untruth banish,
And Evil yield before the Good,
And denigrating Envy vanish
Within the light of Brotherhood.

1ST LADY
[*giving a flute to* TAMINO]
Hail, Prince! Our Queen who favors few,
As favor sends this flute to you.
This magic flute will well defend you
And in your darkest hour befriend you.

LADIES
On moods of doubt and desolation,
Its notes can work a transformation;
The moping soul will dance and sing,
And wintry hearts respond to spring.

ALL

O, this flute has greater worth
Than jeweled crowns or kingdoms, then,
For it can bring good will to men,
Peace, prosperity and mirth,
Good will to all on earth.

PAPAGENO

Lovely nightingales, no doubt you . . .
Want me . . . now to disappear? [*Starts to leave.*]

LADIES

We would gladly do without you
But the Prince requires you here:
He will daunt Sarastro's power
While you find Pamina's bower.

PAPAGENO

Do you want to see me dead!
For Sarastro, you have said,
Is a wild and savage beast,
That without the slightest pity
He would roast me, he would broil me,
He would bake me, he would boil me:
On my bones his dogs will feast!

LADIES

The Prince shall your protector be,
But you must serve him faithfully.

PAPAGENO

The Devil take him: he'll deceive me:
As sure as I draw breath

The Prince'll sneak away and leave me
To be tortured to death.

1ST LADY
[*giving him chimes*]
This, Papageno, is for you.

PAPAGENO
For me? Does it make music, too?

LADIES
Now we will set its bells a-chiming!

PAPAGENO
And can I also set them chiming?

LADIES
The gift is yours, the bells to play.

ALL
Flute and bells have magic powers
To protect you (us) in threatening hours:
So farewell, we must away,
We shall meet another day.

TAMINO
Fair ladies, for one moment stay

PAPAGENO
And tell us how to find our way.
[*The* THREE SPIRITS *enter.*]

LADIES
These pages three shall walk beside you
Along your path to guard you and to guide you.
If you their counsel faithfully obey
Never, O never will you go astray.

TAMINO *and* PAPAGENO
These pages three shall walk beside us
Along our path to guard us and to guide us.
By duty called no longer to remain,
We bid farewell until we meet again.

LADIES
Your duty calls "no more remain."
Farewell, farewell until we meet again.

—————

[TAMINO *and* PAPAGENO, *led by the* THREE SPIRITS, *leave.*]

Scene 11

[PAMINA's *bower: two slaves working.*]

1ST SLAVE
[*hurriedly entering*]
Have you heard? Pamina has escaped!

2ND SLAVE
                              No!

1ST SLAVE
Indeed!

3RD SLAVE
    How happy I am!

2ND SLAVE
                    This will show
Sarastro how Monostatos behaves
To that poor child.

1ST SLAVE
                    I hope he's whipped!

MONOSTATOS
[*off-stage*]
                              Ho! Slaves!

3RD SLAVE
Monostatos!

MONOSTATOS
[*off-stage*]
    Bring chains!

2ND SLAVE
        She has been caught!

1ST SLAVE
And will be chained!

3RD SLAVE
        I cannot bear the thought!
[*The* SLAVES *retire.* MONOSTATOS *enters, dragging* PAMINA
    along with him.]

T R I O

MONOSTATOS
Ah, pretty bird, so white and pure!

PAMINA
How long must I these wrongs endure!

MONOSTATOS
Prepare to die or love me!

PAMINA
No fear of death can move me,
But spare me for my mother's sake:
Her heart of grief and pain would break.

MONOSTATOS
[*to* SLAVES]
Bring chains of steel and manacles!
    [*to* PAMINA]
If you your life still cherish . . . [*Tries to embrace her.*]

PAMINA
[*struggling*]
No, rather let me perish
Than seek to move a heart as hard as stone! [*Faints.*]

MONOSTATOS
[*to* SLAVES]
Go! Go! Away! Leave her with me alone!
[PAPAGENO *peers through a window.*]

PAPAGENO
Well, here I am! I don't know where.
I thought . . . I heard some voices . . .
Dare I? . . . I think I dare! [*Jumps in.*]

On a river bank all alone
I espied a fair pretty maiden . . .
[PAPAGENO *and* MONOSTATOS *catch sight of each other.*]

PAPAGENO *and* MONOSTATOS
Hoo!
It is the devil, without doubt.
Don't touch me! Don't look at me!
Boo!

[*Exeunt,* MONOSTATOS *through door,* PAPAGENO *through window.*]

PAMINA
[*coming to*]
O mother . . . mother . . . hold me . . . where? again
Must I endure the daylight of my pain?

O let me dream! [*Buries her face in her hands.*]

PAPAGENO
[*peering round door*]
                    The jackdaw must have flown.
What's more, there *is* a maiden here. Alone.
Can it be? It could be. She seems young. Sighing.
That's logical. Well, there's no harm in trying.
Excuse me!

PAMINA
          Oh!

PAPAGENO
                    It is! That is, I mean,
You are . . . Pamina, the daughter of Queen
Astrafiammante, aren't you?

PAMINA
                    Alas,
I am. And weep the years that I must pass
Without a mother's love.

PAPAGENO
                    Weep not. You see . . .
Your mother sent me. Well, it's not quite me
She sent. I keep another company.
I'm but an amiable bird-catching zero,
A history of nothing, *he* is a hero,
I, Papageno: he, Prince Tamino.
By visions moved . . . and by your portrait too . . .
He is approaching now to rescue you,
Sent, as I said, by your mother, and spurred—

If you follow—need I mention the word?—
By love, his love for you.

PAMINA

      Love! What happiness!
O tell me, is he near?

PAPAGENO

     I must confess
That, stopping on the way to quench my thirst,
I somehow lost him. [*Aside*] Still, I got here first.
  [*to* PAMINA]
But he should soon be here.

PAMINA

      He will, I know!
And I shall love him! Mother, be thanked!

PAPAGENO
[*starts to cry*]

         O!

PAMINA
Kind Papageno in tears? Tell me why.

PAPAGENO
Your lives and mine contrasted make me cry.
He has a mind in which dreams are created,
That please and that prosper and soon come true;
You have a mother who cares if you're mated,
And kindly arranges the details for you:
I have no family, no mate, no art . . .

PAMINA
All will be well: you have love in your heart.

D U E Tᵇ

PAMINA
When Love in his bosom desire has implanted,
    The heart of the hero grows gentle and tame;

PAPAGENO
And soon from his passion enkindled, enchanted,
    The nymph receives the impetuous flame.

BOTH
      In all our days we mortals can prove
      No greater joy than mutual love.

PAMINA
For Love's dear dominion extends to all nature
    And all to her kindly compulsion must yield;

PAPAGENO
Love solaces every sensible creature,
    The birds in air and the beasts of the field.

BOTH
      The highest goal of Nature's life
      Is the sweet joy of man and wife.
      Man and wife and wife and man
      Follow their Creator's plan.

———————

Scene I I I

[*Outside the gates of the Temple City at sunset. Enter* TAMINO, *led by the* THREE SPIRITS.]

SPIRITS
Your journey's end is now in sight,
Your quest no longer may engage us;
On, on to glory, valiant knight:
Be patient, courteous and courageous.

TAMINO
Immortal children, tell me how
I am to save Pamina now.

SPIRITS
No further we your way can see:
Be patient, courteous and courageous
As knight should be. Faint not nor flee!
On, on to glory, on to victory!
     [*Exeunt* SPIRITS.]

TAMINO
So wise and comforting a counsel ᶜ
Shall be engraved upon my heart.*
Where am I now? What lies before me? *
Is this the dwelling-place of gods?

The pillars, the arches, all seem to bear witness
To Reason and Beauty and Wisdom and Virtue.
Where Greed and Sloth are banished
And Art and Labor reign,
There all the temptations of Vice are in vain.
Now let me be fearless as any true knight,
Defending the helpless, upholding the Right,
To overthrow a tyranny,
To save Pamina, or to die!
    [*Approaches one of the _three_ gates.*]

VOICE
Beware!

TAMINO
"Beware!" "Beware!" I'll try the second door.

VOICE
Beware!

TAMINO
Again the cry "Beware!" I see one opening more.
Am I allowed to enter there?
    [*Gate opens.* PRIEST *appears in the doorway.*]   #3

PRIEST
What purpose, pilgrim, leads you here?
Why have you sought this holy place?

TAMINO
To learn where Love and Virtue dwell.

PRIEST
The words you speak are noble words.
But, friend, what hope have you of learning?

It was not Love that led you here:
Revenge and murder in your heart are burning.

PRIEST

TAMINO

Revenge upon a murderer!

PRIEST

Within this land you will not find him.

TAMINO

But is this not Sarastro's kingdom?

PRIEST

It is; Sarastro is our king.

TAMINO

Not of your holy temple too?

PRIEST

He rules our holy temple too.

TAMINO

Then it is all a painted lie! [*Starts to leave.*]

PRIEST

Are you departing now?

TAMINO

Yes, I will go. Now. At once. Never to see you more!

PRIEST

You speak in ignorance; or you have been deceived.

TAMINO

Sarastro is your king: for me, that is enough!

PRIEST

Now, as you love your life, obey me! Do not move!
You hate Sarastro, then?

TAMINO

I hate, I scorn him, yes!

PRIEST
Can you explain your hate to me?

TAMINO
He is a monster! He is vile!

PRIEST
My son, is what you say well proven?

TAMINO
Well proven by a weeping woman
Whose pure and loving heart he broke!

PRIEST
Whose wiles have well bewitched your mind!
Beware of women: woman's tongue
Can make-believe that foul is fair.
O, could you but Sarastro meet,
You would not doubt his purposes.

TAMINO
His purposes are all too clear.
Did he not steal, did he not ravish
Pamina from her mother's arms? *

PRIEST
He took her from her mother's arms.

TAMINO
Where is she? Fettered and confined?
Or has he made away with her?

PRIEST
Our temple secrets, noble knight,
I am forbidden to reveal.

TAMINO
Enough of riddles! Speak the truth!

PRIEST
My tongue a sacred vow obeys.

TAMINO
When will these clouds of darkness vanish?

PRIEST
As soon as you a vow will swear
Our Holy Brotherhood to share.
[PRIEST *withdraws. Gate closes.*]

TAMINO
O starless night! Unending sorrow!
When, when will come your golden morrow?

VOICES
[*off-stage*]
Soon or never, either—or.

TAMINO
No! No! Torture me not with doubt!
Unfeeling spirits, answer me!
Is Pamina still alive? *

VOICES
[*off-stage*]
Pamina is alive.

TAMINO
Alive! Alive! You turn my night to day!
Tell me with what celestial phrases,
Angelic Ones, to sing your praises!
No tongue has wit that grateful all to utter
That its heart would say.

[*He plays the flute. Wild animals come out to listen.*]
O how soft, enchanting, the magic tone,
Some celestial pleasure voicing;
Such a strain would melt a heart of stone,
Set the creatures in the wilderness rejoicing.
O how soft yet how insistent is the magic tone,
Angelic harmony, celestial pleasure voicing!
Such a strain would melt a heart of stone,
Set the creatures in the wilderness . . . Yes,
But Pamina, but Pamina cannot hear me,
But Pamina does not hear.
Pamina! Pamina! Hear me! Answer me!
Not there. Not there. Where? There? Here?
Alas, my love is nowhere near.
[*Pan-pipes heard as an echo to his flute off-stage.*]
Ah! I hear a familiar sound!
Can it mean Pamina has been found?
Can it mean that she is waiting there?
Could it be? It could be already she is waiting there.
[*Exit.*]

Scene I V

[*An open court within the City. In the background a temple with great bronze doors. Enter* PAPAGENO *and* PAMINA *in flight.*]

PAPAGENO *and* PAMINA
Walk on tiptoe! Hold your breath!
To be captured would mean a painful death.
All about are watchful eyes
Who would catch us, who would catch us in a trice.

PAMINA
Tamino!

PAPAGENO
　　Softer, softer, softer! I know something better.
[*Plays his pipes.* TAMINO'*s flute is heard in answer.*]

PAPAGENO *and* PAMINA
O for friends what joy is greater,
O what pleasure more complete,
Than for parted friends to meet
And relate what they have seen and done:
Let us hurry, hurry, hurry, let us run.* ᵈ
　　[*Enter* MONOSTATOS *with* SLAVES.]

MONOSTATOS
Let us hurry, hurry, hurry, let us run! *
Now! . . . Now we shall have some fun!

Into irons I mean to throw you,
A good lesson need to show you:
All my kindness proved an error,
I shall tame you now by terror!
    [*to* SLAVES]
Bring me chains to bind them with!

    PAPAGENO *and* PAMINA
All is done and over with!

    PAPAGENO
Now it's all, all or nothing, I know well:
Chime, my pretty silver bell!
Let all ears be now enchanted,
Dreaming that their dreams are granted.
    [*He plays.* MONOSTATOS *and* SLAVES *dance away en-
    chanted.*]

    MONOSTATOS *and* SLAVES
Let us follow the music, let us caper away!
    Fa la la
Over mountain and valley to dance night and day.
    Fa la la.
    [*Exeunt* MONOSTATOS *and* SLAVES.]

    PAPAGENO *and* PAMINA
Friends who such a music make
    Cannot be divided;
Anger to his heels will take,
    Fear cannot abide it.

Music makes us frank and free,
Joined in peaceful harmony.

Rich men, poor men, all agree,
    So do men of learning,
Music, Love and Sympathy
    Keep our green world turning.
    [*From within the temple comes the sound of singing.*]

CHORUS
[*within*]
Give praise to Sarastro, devoutly praise him!

PAPAGENO
What's that? What's that pudder?
I shiver, I shudder.

PAMINA
Too late! Too late! I hear the drums
Announcing that Sarastro comes.

PAPAGENO
O would I were a mouse
Safe in the church's keeping,
A snail securely sleeping
Inside his tiny house!
But now . . . now what are we to say? *

PAMINA
The Truth now, Truth, let come what may! * ᵉ
    [*The temple doors open and out comes a procession pre-
       ceding* SARASTRO, *flanked by* 1ST *and* 2ND PRIESTS.]

CHORUS
Give praise to Sarastro, devoutly adore him,
The proud and ungodly lie prostrate before him:
His word is redeeming, his counsels are wise;
Let praise of Sarastro ascend to the skies.

PAMINA
[*kneeling before* SARASTRO]
Ah! Guilty at your feet I lie,
Who from your kingdom sought to fly.
Not all the guilt falls on my head:
Your traitor liege would have compelled me
To loveless love: therefore I fled.

SARASTRO
Arise and weep no more, Pamina!
I, too, the truth alone would tell you,
The secret of whose heart I know.
There is a name already written on your heart:
He commands your heart.
To love I never will compel you,
But still I may not let you go.

PAMINA
A daughter's longing bade me go
To see my mother.

SARASTRO
                              Child, you do not know
How warped and loveless you would grow
Were I to leave you in her keeping.

PAMINA
Yet still for her my eyes are weeping.

SARASTRO
Passion rules her life.
A man must rule your education:
Without man's guidance women grow too vain and proud,
Forget their station.
          [*Enter* MONOSTATOS *with captured* TAMINO.]

MONOSTATOS

Down, down, young man, upon your knees:
Sarastro's frown your blood will freeze.

    [TAMINO *and* PAMINA *catch sight of each other and fly
        into each other's arms.*]

TAMINO *and* PAMINA

'Tis He! 'Tis She! But do I dream?
'Tis She! 'Tis He! I do not dream.
Within his (her) fond embraces, I
Both death and torment will defy.

CHORUS

Mountains and Marvels!

MONOSTATOS

                Shameless and insolent!
Let go before I strike you! For this you shall repent!

    [MONOSTATOS *comes forward and kneels before* SARAS-
        TRO.]

My Lord, I bring you information,
Against this youth lay accusation,
Who with audacity unheard,
Assisted by this artful bird [*pointing to* PAPAGENO]
Of Fair Pamina tried to rob you
And would have done, had I not stopped him . . .
My service . . . My deserts you know.

SARASTRO

For these a recompense I owe.
Toward your just reward shall go . . .

MONOSTATOS

Your favor sets my heart aglow!

S A R A S T R O
Full seventy with the bastinado.

M O N O S T A T O S
Ah, no! How can you treat your servant so!

S A R A S T R O
Away! Or I my wrath will show.

C H O R U S
Give praise to Sarastro, give glory and praise,*
For just are his dealings and righteous his ways.* *

S A R A S T R O
Cover their faces piously, their feet toward the temple guide.
None may our sacred rites behold until he has been purified.

> [*The* 1ST PRIEST *takes charge of* TAMINO, *the* 2ND *of*
> PAPAGENO. *The procession retires toward the temple,*
> SARASTRO *with* PAMINA, *followed by* 1ST PRIEST *with*
> TAMINO *and* 2ND *with* PAPAGENO. *As they reach the*
> *doors,* PAPAGENO *tries to bolt, but is firmly held by the*
> 2ND PRIEST. *The doors close behind them.*]

C H O R U S
To Justice and to Righteousness
We pray, that soon may come the day
When Truth shall be revealed to all
And every vain idol fall.

[*Curtain*]

Metalogue

[*To be spoken by the singer taking the rôle of* SARASTRO.]

Relax, Maestro, put your baton down:
Only the fogiest of the old will frown
If you the trials of the Prince *prorogue*
To let Sarastro *speak the Metalogue,*
A form acceptable to us, although
Unclassed by Aristotle *or* Boileau.
No modern audience finds it incorrect,
For interruption is what we expect,
Since that new god, the Paid Announcer, rose
Who with his quasi-Ossianic prose
Cuts in upon the lovers, halts the band
To name a sponsor or to praise a brand.
Not that I have a product to describe
That you could wear or cook with or imbibe;
You cannot hoard or waste a work of art:
I come to praise but not to sell Mozart,

Who came into this world of war and woe
At Salzburg just two centuries ago,
When kings were many and machines were few
And open Atheism something new.
(It makes a servantless New Yorker sore
To think sheer Genius had to stand before
A mere Archbishop with uncovered head:
But Mozart never had to make his bed.)

The history of Music as of Man
Will not go cancrizans, and no ear can
Recall what, when the Archduke Francis reigned,
Was heard by ears whose treasure-hoard contained
A Flute already but as yet no Ring:
Each age has its own mode of listening.
We know the Mozart of our fathers' time
Was gay, rococo, sweet, but not sublime,
A Viennese Italian: that is changed
Since music-critics learned to feel "estranged";
Now it's the Germans he is class amongst,
A Geist whose music was composed from Angst,
At International Festivals enjoys
An equal status with the Twelve-Tone Boys;
He awes the lovely and the very rich,
And even those Divertimenti which
He wrote to play while bottles were uncorked,
Milord chewed noisily, Milady talked,
Are heard in solemn silence, score on knees,
Like quartets by the deafest of the B's.

What next? One can no more imagine how,
In concert halls two hundred years from now,
When the Mozartian sound waves move the air,
The cognoscenti will be moved than dare
Predict how high orchestral pitch will go,
How many tones will constitute a row,
The tempo at which regimented feet
Will march about the Moon, the form of suite
For piano in a Post-Atomic Age,
Prepared by some contemporary Cage.

An opera composer may be vexed
By later umbrage taken at his text:
{ *Even* Macaulay's *schoolboy knows today*
  What Robert Graves *or* Margaret Mead *would say* }
  About the status of the sexes in this play,
Writ in that era of barbaric dark
'Twixt Modern Mom and Bronze-Age Matriarch.
Where now the Roman Fathers and their creed?
"Ah, where," sighs Mr. Mitty, *"where indeed?"*
And glances sideways at his vital spouse
Whose rigid jaw-line and contracted brows
Express her scorn and utter detestation
For Roman views on Female Education.
In Nineteen Fifty-six we find the Queen
A highly paid and most efficient Dean
(Who, as we all know, really runs the College),
Sarastro, *tolerated for his knowledge,*
Teaching the History of Ancient Myth

At Bryn Mawr, Vassar, Bennington *or* Smith;
Pamina *may a* Time *researcher be*
To let Tamino *take his Ph.D.,*
Acquiring manly wisdom as he wishes
While changing diapers and doing dishes;
Sweet Papagena, *when she's time to spare,*
Listens to Mozart *operas on the air,*
Though Papageno, *one is sad to feel,*
Prefers the juke-box to the glockenspiel,
And how is—what was easy in the past—
A democratic villain to be cast?
Monostatos *must make his bad impression*
Without a race, religion or profession.

A work that lives two hundred years is tough,
And operas, God knows, must stand enough:
What greatness made, small vanities abuse.
What must they not endure? The Diva whose
Fioriture *and climactic note*
The silly old composer never wrote,
Conductor X, that overrated bore,
Who alters tempi and who cuts the score,
Director Y who with ingenious wit
Places the wretched singers in the pit
While dancers mime their roles, Z the Designer
Who sets the whole thing on an ocean liner,
The girls in shorts, the man in yachting caps,
Yet genius triumphs over all mishaps,
Survives a greater obstacle than these,

Translation into foreign Operese.
(*English sopranos are condemned to* languish
Because our tenors have to hide their anguish.)
It soothes the Frank, *it stimulates the* Greek:
Genius surpasses all things, even chic.
We who know little—which is just as well—
About the future can, at least, foretell,
Whether they live in air-borne nylon cubes,
Practice group-marriage or are fed through tubes,
That crowds, two centuries from now, will press
(*Absurd their hair, ridiculous their dress*),
And pay in currencies however weird
To hear Sarastro *booming through his beard,*
Sharp connoisseurs approve if it is clean
The F in alt of the nocturnal Queen,
Some uncouth creature from the Bronx *amaze*
Park Avenue *by knowing all the K's.*

How seemly, then, to celebrate the birth
Of one who did no harm to our poor earth,
Created masterpieces by the dozen,
Indulged in toilet humor with his cousin,
And had a pauper's funeral in the rain,
The like of whom we shall not see again;
How comely, also, to forgive: we should,
As Mozart, *were he living, surely would,*
Remember kindly Salieri's *shade,*
Accused of murder and his works unplayed,
Nor, while we praise the dead, should we forget

We have Stravinsky, *bless him, with us yet.*
Basta! *Maestro, make your minions play!*
In all hearts, as in our finale, may
Reason and Love be crowned, assume their rightful sway.

ACT TWO

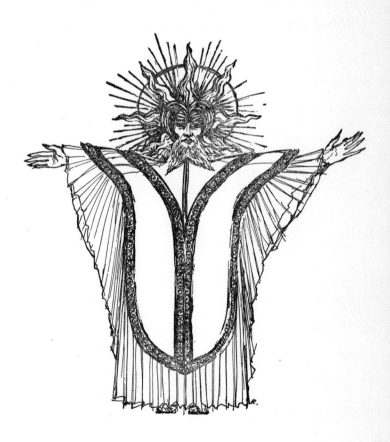

Sarastro

Scene I

[*A hall in the Temple City of the Sun.*]

SARASTRO
A joyful purpose and occasion dear
Have brought us, brethren, to assemble here:
The High Prince, avid of the highest good,
Desires to join our Holy Brotherhood.
Let him approach.
　　　[*Three trumpet blasts.* TAMINO *is led forward by* 1ST
　　　PRIEST.]
　　　　　　　　Prince, knowing what you speak
The gods will hear, confess the goal you seek:
What does your mind desire, your heart demand?

TAMINO
The light of Wisdom and Pamina's hand.

SARASTRO
Are you prepared to risk your life for these
And lose them both if so the gods should please?

TAMINO
I am.

SARASTRO
Do you, Tamino, choose of your free will
To face the rites that purify or kill?

TAMINO

I do.

SARASTRO

Will you, without complaining or delay,
The orders of the Brotherhood obey?

TAMINO

I will.

SARASTRO

Escort him hence; in ways of holiness
Instruct him further: pray for his success.

[*Exeunt* TAMINO *and* 1ST PRIEST.]

A R I A   A N D   C H O R U S

SARASTRO

O Isis and Osiris, hear him,
    Accept this vow that he has made,
In hours of trial and grief be near him,
    Comfort his heart when sore afraid,
    And guide him through the dreadful shade.

May love be born of tribulation,
    Show him the path to his salvation,
And when this mortal life shall cease,
    From vain desire the soul release,
    Grant him your everlasting peace.

Scene 11

[*A large hall in the Temple of the Sun.*]

PAPAGENO
[*to* 2ND PRIEST]
No thank you, no: I overheard
The whole proceedings word by word.
Does Papageno choose of his free will
To face the rites that purify or kill?
I don't!
Will he without complaining or delay,
The orders of the Brotherhood obey?
I won't!
What does his mind desire, his heart demand?
Good food, good drink, a girl who's not too grand,
A girl whom he can understand,
Someone like me.

2ND PRIEST
          Supposing such a maid,
Some rose-cheeked, tender, merry-hearted maid,
Called Papagena, shall we say, should be
Awaiting you . . .

PAPAGENO
          Lucky her and happy me!

Where is she? Let me see her!

2ND PRIEST

Suppose, I said.

PAPAGENO

[*aside*]

I know her smile and how she tilts her head!

2ND PRIEST

To marry if you choose . . .

PAPAGENO

Of course I choose.

2ND PRIEST

The way of trial.

PAPAGENO

The way where I might lose

My life?

2ND PRIEST

That way.

PAPAGENO

Supposing I refuse.

2ND PRIEST

You'll never meet her.

PAPAGENO

Never?

2ND PRIEST

Never.

PAPAGENO

Then,

Supposing friend, you must suppose again:

I'll remain single. Ah, the Prince at last!

[*Enter* TAMINO *and* 1ST PRIEST.]
My Prince, my dear good friend, why choose so fast?
There must be other means by which to gain
Wisdom and Love without such toil and pain.

TAMINO
No, Papageno, there's no other way.

PAPAGENO
That's only what you've heard Sarastro say.
You think him honest?

TAMINO
                    That is my belief.

PAPAGENO
How honest when Sarastro is a thief?

2ND PRIEST
Beware, rash fool, and hold your tongue!

PAPAGENO
                                    He took
Both flute and bells away: then, by the Book,
He stole them for they were not his but ours.

1ST PRIEST
Till purified from all unhallowed powers
These instruments could work you harm and sorrow:
Sarastro will return them both tomorrow.

PAPAGENO
Sarastro says.

2ND PRIEST
            Sarastro never lies.

PAPAGENO
[*aside*]
Ergo, Sarastro is not always wise.

1ST PRIEST
[*to* TAMINO]
The sun has set; the night comes on apace,
And Night is the first trial you must face,
The lying voices of the dark to hear,
The cries of lust, doubt, accusation, fear.
For which in preparation listen to our teaching.

PAPAGENO
No nightmare could be worse than old men preaching.

D U E T

PRIESTS
A woman's heart on manly reason
    Its ardent Virtue can bestow,
Unless man make of warmth a treason,
    Conspiring Virtue's overthrow.

For Lust, that treacherous deceiver
    Can counterfeit the sacred flame,
But then betrays the fond believer,
    Leaves him to self-reproach and shame.

―――――

[*The lights start to dim, the* PRIESTS *to leave.*]

PAPAGENO

I'll come with you. No trials, please, for me.
No power can compel me.

2ND PRIEST

You are free

To be without me.

[*Door shuts behind them. Total darkness.*]

PAPAGENO

But it's dark! I won't!

Don't leave me! Let me out! Help! I'm betrayed!
Where is your hand, Tamino? I'm afraid.

Q U I N T E T

LADIES

[*appearing suddenly*]

Why? Why? Why
Do you rashly linger on?
Fly! Fly! Fly
From your peril and be gone!
This teeming pit of deadly error
Is monstrous with deforming terror.

PAPAGENO

This I find alarming news!

TAMINO

I continue as I choose.
Their pretended trepidation
Is but folly and temptation.

PAPAGENO

But are you certain you are right?

TAMINO

Hold your tongue and do not fear!

PAPAGENO

Do not talk and do not hear
And do not there and do not here!

LADIES

Prophetic creatures of the night,
We know the dreadful doom in sight.

PAPAGENO

What doom? Is it avoidable?

TAMINO

Do not hear them, and be still!
Or you never will attain a
Rank deserving Papagena.

LADIES

Believe not here what may be sworn you:
Where all is false, can vows be made?
The Queen who sent us here to warn you,
You have, for lying words, betrayed.

TAMINO

Who has the light of wisdom seen
Will not avow your vengeful Queen,
Nor be misled, nor be afraid.

LADIES

The love you shall not win is dear,
For with your lives you pay the price!

PAPAGENO

So then if I fulfill each trifle here
And stifle fear,

No wife'll still appear!
Then wifeless, lifeless? Is that nice?

TAMINO
Believe not those to whom the breath
Of Love and Wisdom speak of Death!

PAPAGENO
But if the Queen says we shall die?

TAMINO
Her passions drive the Queen to lie.
And you are driving me away!
If you go on, I shall not stay!

LADIES
Why yearn for love when we are pleasant,
Compliant, unattached . . . and present?

PAPAGENO
[*aside to* LADIES]
You mustn't think me rude . . .

TAMINO
                                        Stop!

PAPAGENO
[*aside to* LADIES]
But threats of solitude . . .

TAMINO
                                        Stop!

TAMINO *and* PAPAGENO
A man must learn how to be lonely
Although the discipline be hard.

LADIES
What can we do if they will only
Ignore us in their self-regard?

TAMINO *and* PAPAGENO
What can they do if we will only
Ignore them and their self-regard?

ALL
In bright formalities of art,
In fearful shadows of the heart,
With open manner, open eyes,
With stratagem and mean disguise,

1ST *and* 2ND LADIES
Alas, that even in our lies,

TAMINO, PAPAGENO *and* 3RD LADY
A man can study to be wise:

1ST *and* 2ND LADIES
Though soon by our revenge he dies,

TAMINO, PAPAGENO *and* 3RD LADY
A man can study to be wise.

CHORUS
[*off-stage*]
Brave Chanticleer crows up the morning,
To spirits of darkness a warning.

LADIES
Away! Away! Away!
[*They flee.*]

PAPAGENO
I die! I faint! I fai . . . (1)! [*Falls to the ground.*]

———————

[*Dawn*]

TAMINO

Papageno, Papageno, open your eyes.
Already morning brightens in the skies
And all is over.

PAPAGENO

       Have those witches gone?

TAMINO

Yes.

PAPAGENO

    Promise?

TAMINO

      Yes. Get up!

PAPAGENO

        I daren't.

TAMINO

         Come on!

PAPAGENO

[*getting up*]

What a nightmare! Tamino, weren't you frightened?

TAMINO

I was.

PAPAGENO

    But then you want to be enlightened,
I don't. I'm cold. I'm hungry. Why, why, why
Did I leave my cosy hut? My birds will die.
I want to go home.

TAMINO

      But not without a wife.

PAPAGENO
I've never been so hungry in my life.
O that I had the bells Sarastro took!
My! What a spread I'd conjure.

TAMINO
Listen! Look!
[*Enter the* THREE SPIRITS *with food, wine and the flute
and bells.*]

T R I O

SPIRITS
So for the second time we meet you,
This time where grave Sarastro dwells;
He has commanded us to greet you
And to return your flute and bells.

Also with food we may provide you;
Eat, then, and drink to your content:
May we a third time stand beside you,
Join in your feasting and merriment.

Tamino, forth: Well fares your quest.
Back, Papageno: Safety is the best.

———————

[*Exeunt* SPIRITS.]

PAPAGENO
Wine is a friend with whom I never quarrel;

He warms my spirits and he points no moral.
Were I in search of wisdom I should look
Not to Sarastro but Sarastro's cook.
Tamino, tell me, do you still intend
To face these trials to the very end?

TAMINO
I must be faithful to my chosen fate.

PAPAGENO
I feared so. Then our paths must separate.

TAMINO
But still as friends we'll walk them. May each find
The honor that is proper to his kind.
To each his mystery: the gods bless all! [*Drinks.*]

PAPAGENO
The gods bless birds and maidens, one and all! [*Drinks.*]
    [*Enter the* TWO PRIESTS.]
Here come our bearded elders: mine looks glum.

1ST PRIEST
Hail, Prince, who have so bravely overcome
The night's alarms; we hail your victory.
Sarastro is well pleased.

PAPAGENO
                    But not with me.

2ND PRIEST
[*to* PAPAGENO]
You, feather-witted clod of common clay,
Have leave to go your own unworthy way.

PAPAGENO
Long live Sarastro! And, dear Prince, farewell.

Let common clay turn prophet. I foretell
Pamina shall be yours.

TAMINO

Farewell, good friend,
And may we meet together at the end.

PAPAGENO

And all be feasting and fun. [*To* 2ND PRIEST] Come, my old
supposer,
Lead me to Papagena and disclose her.

    [*Exeunt* PAPAGENO *and* 2ND PRIEST.]

1ST PRIEST

Courageous Prince, I must prepare you now
To face your second trial. You must vow
Yourself to silence; henceforth you may speak
With none but your instructors and in meek
Obedience hold your tongue, appear to all
Both deaf and dumb, responding to no call,
No cry, no offer, order or request
By friend or foe. Beware, Tamino, lest
Pity or love betray you. You must keep
This vow no matter who may sigh and weep
For just one word, whose loving heart mistake
Your silence for indifference and break.

TAMINO

I will endure this for Pamina's sake.

1ST PRIEST

The gods be with you! [*Exit* 1ST PRIEST. PAPAGENO *peers*
round the corner.]

PAPAGENO
[*aside*]
                    Virtue quits the scene,
[*to* TAMINO]
Tamino! Tamino! O what fools we've been.
We've got our flute and bells back. They will find
Pamina for you. Quickly! Never mind
Sarastro and his trials! Come with me!
Tamino! Are you deaf? Ah, now I see!
Hm, hm, hm, hm, hm, hm, hm.
Fancy a Prince, so anxious to be wise
Struck dumb like me, a Prince caught telling lies!
    [*sings*]
    By words I can express my pity
    But that is all my words can do.ᵍ
    Hm, hm, hm, hm.

PAMINA
[*off-stage*]
Tamino!

PAPAGENO
    Though I'm not a clever bird
I do know better than to make a third
When lovers meet. Take wing!

    [*Exit* PAPAGENO *as* PAMINA *enters.*]

PAMINA
                    My love, how long
The time has been without you.
                    What is wrong?

My love, Tamino, do you know me not?
Pamina speaks to you.

Have I been forgot

So soon?

Do you love me no more?

O say

You love me still!

Tamino!

See! I pray

[*kneels*]
Your grace.

I love you.

Love!

He turns away.

A R I A

PAMINA
Hearts may break though grief be silent,
True hearts make their love their lives,
Silence love with ended lives:
Love that dies in one false lover
Kills the heart where love survives.

O Tamino, see the silence
Of my tears betray my grief,
Faithful grief: if you flee
My love in silence, in faithless silence,
Let my sorrow die with me.

If you can betray Pamina,
If you love me not, Tamino,
Let my sorrow die with me,
  And silent be.

———————

  [*As* PAMINA *is leaving,* SARASTRO *enters and leads her
   gently back.*]

   SARASTRO
Prince, for the last time, do you still desire
To face the test by water and by fire?
If you have changed your mind, you still are free
To go no further.

   PAMINA
      Tamino, stay with me.

   SARASTRO
From former promise or from future task
I will straightway release you if you ask.

   PAMINA
Ask, for my sake, before it is too late!

   SARASTRO
Speak, then.

   TAMINO
     I reaffirm my chosen fate.

   SARASTRO
Then for your trial you must now prepare
With study, fasting, solitude and prayer,
Forsaking beauty for a hermit's cell.

   PAMINA
Do not forsake me!

SARASTRO
   Bid this world farewell . . .

PAMINA
Beloved, stay!

SARASTRO
    As one who knows not when,
If ever, he will see its face again.

T R I O

PAMINA
[*to* TAMINO]
O we shall never meet again!

SARASTRO
[*aside*]
In triumph they shall meet again.

PAMINA
[*to* TAMINO]
For death, not love, is your election.

TAMINO *and* SARASTRO
I (he) trust(s) the gods and their protection.

PAMINA
[*to* TAMINO]
Your peril, say my premonitions,
Is greater, deadlier than you know.

TAMINO
[*aside*]
The gods decree without conditions,
And where they bid me, there I go.

SARASTRO
[*to* PAMINA]
The gods decree without conditions
And where they bid, there he must go.

PAMINA
You would not act in such a fashion
If you felt love as deep as mine.

TAMINO *and* SARASTRO
[*aside*]
I (he) feel(s) no less profound a passion
And would my (his) life for her resign.

PAMINA
[*to* TAMINO]
O bitter grief of parting!
Tamino, why must you be gone?
Why must you go, Tamino?
O golden morning, dawn so beautiful,
Soon return, let all be well!

TAMINO
[*aside*]
O bitter grief of parting!
Pamina, I must now be gone.
I have to go, Pamina.
O golden morning, dawn so beautiful,
Soon return, let all be well!

SARASTRO
[*to* PAMINA]
The hour strikes; he must be starting.

64

[*to* TAMINO]
Tamino, you must now be gone.
    [*to* PAMINA]
He has to go.
    [*to* TAMINO]
You must away, no more delay, Tamino!
    [*aside*]
The hour strikes! His Quest will end well!

———————

[*Exeunt* TAMINO *and* SARASTRO.]

PAMINA
Tamino! [*Weeps.*]
    [*Enter* PAPAGENO]
    PAPAGENO
      Papagena! Papage . . . [*Seeing* PAMINA]
                No!
Not in tears again! Love's a dreadful woe.
Perhaps it's just as well I never find
Her who engages heart and soul and mind . . .
Or such mind as I have . . . If Love have in it
Such power to distress my lovely linnet. [*Goes to* PAMINA.]
Pamina, dear!
    PAMINA
      Tamino!
    PAPAGENO
        Please! A tear
In a woman's eye unnerves me. Please, my dear,

Don't cry! I'm sure it's not his fault. The best
Advice, I know, seems heartless. Try to rest.
It's all Sarastro's doing, crazy man!
I wish that I could help. Perhaps I can.
　　[*Takes his chimes and sings.*] ʰ
Go to sleep, do not weep,
Go to sleep where all is well:
Listen to the silver bell!
Let your ears be now enchanted,
Dreaming that your dream is granted.
　　[PAMINA *falls asleep.*]

2ND PRIEST
[*off-stage*]
Papageno! Hither, fool!

PAPAGENO
[*aside*]
　　　　　　　My learned owl!
More lessons!

2ND PRIEST
　　Come!

PAPAGENO
[*loudly to* PRIEST]
　　　　　I come, sagacious fowl.
　　[*Exit* PAPAGENO. *Enter* MONOSTATOS.]

MONOSTATOS
Now here's a chance too good to miss! My lot
Has quite improved to send me this. By what
Sweet luck is she alone, asleep? A kiss? Why not?

A R I A

MONOSTATOS

Every animal and human
Comes on earth to make a pair;
For each man there is a woman,
So, should anybody care
If I take my little share?
With a kiss I will but sample
What all people take and I
Must not to myself deny.
With all Nature for example,
Why should ugliness be shy?

And her beauty in relation
To my ugliness is right:
In the order of creation
Only opposites excite
The contrasting appetite.
She is frank and I am scheming,
I am warm and she is cold;
She is young and I am old,
I'm awake and she is dreaming:
So, Monostatos, be bold!

[MONOSTATOS *creeps stealthily toward the sleeping*
PAMINA. *Thunder and lightning.* ASTRAFIAMMANTE
and the THREE LADIES *appear suddenly. The* QUEEN
stands immobile, in her hand a dagger.] [1]

3RD LADY
Back!

[MONOSTATOS *jumps back and cowers in a corner.*
PAMINA *wakes, leaps to her feet, startled, and then,
with arms outstretched, runs toward her mother.*]

PAMINA
Mother, I . . .

3RD LADY
[*intercepting her*]
                    The Queen is not pleased.

1ST LADY
Her heart is in pain.

2ND LADY
                    She would have it eased
By proofs of your devotion.

[ASTRAFIAMMANTE *hands dagger to* 1ST LADY, *who hands
it to* PAMINA.]

1ST LADY
                    In your hands
She places this.

2ND LADY
                    A daughter understands
The gift.

3RD LADY
          Sarastro dies!

PAMINA
                    Dies!

3RD LADY
                    Silence! She commands.

A R I A

ASTRAFIAMMANTE
Avenging fury lacerates my spirit,
Rage at Sarastro darkly throbs and wild
Blood cries for blood, O may my own blood hear it!
Impale his heart or you are not my child.

Sarastro has betrayed me! Tamino now betrays me:
My daughter would betray me and a mother's love deny.
Tormented, impassioned Nature sways me
As the heartless I defy!
My pain is deep, Sarastro's blood allays me:
Swear! Swear! Swear to avenge me! Or accursèd die!

———————

[ASTRAFIAMMANTE *and the* LADIES *disappear.*]
PAMINA
[*wildly*]
Dies. Who shall die? Kill. Who shall kill? O why
Does all the love I know command me: Die?
Merciful gods!
MONOSTATOS
[*coming up softly behind her*]
Give your love to me.
PAMINA
You!
MONOSTATOS
Or would you rather that Sarastro knew
What you have been commanded? Come, my sweet,

Refusal would be very indiscreet.

PAMINA
Never!

MONOSTATOS
You force me then . . .

SARASTRO
[*entering*]

Who speaks of force?

MONOSTATOS
[*immediately kneeling*]
My lord, if you but knew . . .

SARASTRO

I know the source

Of your concern.

MONOSTATOS
My love for you.

SARASTRO
Your lust

For one I placed unwisely in your trust.
The gods forgive me!
O vile! that with your soul corrupt your dust
Which might, without a soul, have found the good
Of animals, at least. With brotherhood,
Our Holy Order, we had hoped to win
Your mind and soul from what we found them in—
A savage state; but you are of the lost:
Like the enfeebled asp, undone by frost,
Some kindly peasant puts before his fire
Only to find that light and warmth inspire

A graceless nature to renew its venomed ire.
Enough! I banish you! If you are seen
Within these walls again: Death!

MONOSTATOS
[exiting; aside]

To the Queen!

SARASTRO
[sadly]
Then Wisdom must use force: that is the worst.
[to PAMINA]
My dear child—

PAMINA
[clutching the dagger to her breast; wildly]
Come not near! I am accurs'd!
[She runs out.]

SARASTRO
Spirits of Good, protect the noble child!
[Pause, then reflectively]
Spirits of Good . . . and, still unreconciled,
Spirits of Evil. Day and night. And all
Our forces wage a war perpetual.
I have grown old in combat, and I fear
Passionless. Can Wisdom be too dear?
Can she, the Queen of superstitious Night,
In her extremities of heart, be right?
No, no. We need each other. May we learn
Of music how to serve each other's turn:
For music, from the primal darkness sprung,
Speaks an undifferentiating tongue,

But tamed by harmony, the beast can tame,
And every elemental passion name.
  [*He lifts his hands in invocation.*]
O light of Wisdom, do not blind our eyes:
That Mind may love, and Heart may civilize.
  [*He brings his hands down and lowers his head in
  prayer.*]

A R I A

SARASTRO
In holy rites, in labor,
  We join and learn to bear
The burden of our neighbor,
  His joys and woes to share.
He who forgives another's wrong
Shall hear the stars' triumphant song,
He who another's need supplies
Already dwells in Paradise.

By freeing one another
  We learn ourselves to free,
For man must love his brother
  Or cease a man to be.
The homely shepherds when they love
A green and social pasture rove,
The tyrant on his golden throne
Dwells in a desert all alone.

[*Enter* 1ST *and* 2ND PRIESTS.]

1ST PRIEST

Sire!
The charge you laid upon me is fulfilled.
Never before so apt, so eager-willed
A novice have I taught. My years of learning
He compassed into hours, and with such discerning
Questions searched out my understanding that
Soon at his feet a doting pupil sat.

SARASTRO

How as a lover has he borne our ban,
The absence of Pamina?

1ST PRIEST

                    Like a man
He hides his grief; but I have heard him groan
At moments when he thought himself alone,
Who, when he saw me, smiled as if no care
Had ever touched him.

SARASTRO

                  It is well. Prepare
The Caves of Fire and Water, and with songs
Escort him to the test for which he longs.

[*Exit* 1ST PRIEST.]

2ND PRIEST

What of the silly bird-catcher, my lord?
He cannot, will not learn.

SARASTRO

                  Let his reward
Be Papagena.

2ND PRIEST
[*shocked*]
      But . . .

SARASTRO
           If you see fit
That he to some ordeal should submit,
Let this be trifling. He, too, is a child of grace
Who knows his nature and who keeps his place.
    [*Exit* 2ND PRIEST. SARASTRO *comes forward and addresses the audience.*]

SARASTRO
Now my task is almost done:
When tomorrow's rising sun
Sees the Queen of Night's defeat
Shall my mission be complete,
And in that victorious hour
I must also lose my power,
Gratefully my throne resign
To a happier strength than mine.
In one wedding Day and Night,
Light and Darkness shall unite,
And their long wars ended be
In a mutual sympathy:
Blessing them, may I be blest,
Bid this world farewell and rest.

Scene III

[*A grove; sundown. In the background a procession of priests winds through the trees, escorting* TAMINO *to the Trials. In the foreground, watching it pass, stand* PAPAGENO *and the* 2ND PRIEST.]

C H O R U S

CHORUS
O Isis and Osiris, great and gracious,
The pathless shade inform with light sagacious
When all the unchecked elements deride him,
Down through their realm of hostile chaos guide him:
    Inspire his heart, instruct his youth,
       Soon, soon,
    May he be soon reborn in truth,
       Light and truth.[j]

PAPAGENO
Well, aren't you glad that you're not in his shoes?

2ND PRIEST
I wish that I were worthy.

PAPAGENO
               What's the use
Of trying to make friends? Once in a while
You might relax and even laugh or smile.

2ND PRIEST
[*sadly*]
Laughter does not become me, I am told.
Some of the Brethren say I'm getting old.
I know I can't read quickly. I'm not clever.
But they needn't keep on sneering. [*Sniffs.*]

PAPAGENO
                                        Well, I never!
How stupid of me! But who would have thought
That you, at heart, were Papageno's sort?
Laugh at them! Look at me! I cannot spell
But I can find my way about as well
As any Brother. I trust my eyes and nose
To know a fungus from a guelder-rose.

2ND PRIEST
[*pulling himself together*]
Beware, young man, beware! The louder the boast
The harder the fall.

PAPAGENO
                    We're back!

2ND PRIEST
                                        I have been most
Remiss. I beg you to forget my indiscretion.
We were discussing . . .

PAPAGENO
                        Not another session!

2ND PRIEST
What is the Good?

PAPAGENO
>The Good would now be wine,
If wine there were.

> [PRIEST *claps his hands. A slave appears with wine and
> exits.*]

2ND PRIEST
[*nostalgically*]
>Tell me, is it a mere sign
Or does it participate in the Divine?

PAPAGENO
This is a day of wonders without end,
The wine delicious, you my dear new friend.
Let's drink confusion to all fools who read.
Where is your glass?

2ND PRIEST
>Water is all I need.
Fermented juices of whatever kind
Inflame the passions and perturb the mind.

PAPAGENO
But that is what we take them for.

2ND PRIEST
>I know.
I was notorious many years ago
As an imbiber.

PAPAGENO
>Bless you, ancient Druid. [*Drinks.*]

2ND PRIEST
I'll leave you now to your pernicious fluid.

> [*Exit* 2ND PRIEST.]

PAPAGENO

What a day! I feel so strange. I'd like to fly
Up like a lark, up, up into the sky,
Singing, singing of . . . Virtue? Surely not.
Of money? I don't think so. Then . . . of what?

A R I A

PAPAGENO

Could I but once discover
    Some soft congenial She,
How kindly would I love her
    And how happy I should be.
My heart it would glow like a taper,
How nimbly my two legs would caper.
If such were to happen I would
Be always exceedingly good.

If, like in dreams and fancies,
    Some soft congenial She
Would throw me tender glances
    O how happy I should be.
A maid is the crown of creation
But none look at me with elation.
I never can find one to wed,
O sometimes I wish I were dead.

If maiden or if matron,
    Some soft congenial She,

Would take me for her patron,
      O how happy I should be.
My body grows thin as a cleaver,
I'm wasting away with a fever;
I'm half in the grave as it is,
But I could be cured by a kiss.

———————

[*to be spoken alla battuta.*]

PAPAGENO

Heartless gods! Must I remain alone?
      [*Enter* PAPAGENA, *disguised as an old woman.*]
                              Who's *this*? What shall
   I say?
Though she's not my Papagena, still she's company. Good
   day!

PAPAGENA

I am looking for my true love. Do you know where he can be?

PAPAGENO

Does the gentleman that *you* love know that your true love
   is he?

PAPAGENA

No, he doesn't but he *will* know. Do you seek your true love
   too?

PAPAGENO

Yes, I do but I have still no notion where she is. Have you?

PAPAGENA

Does the maiden you love truly know that truly you love her?

PAPAGENO

No, not yet but she will duly when our meeting can occur.

PAPAGENA

If you ask me more I *may* know how to show you when to
meet.

PAPAGENO

And if *you* help Papageno, he may help you find *your* sweet.
Does he want to be your lover?

PAPAGENA

Yes, but doesn't know it yet.

PAPAGENO

When will he his love discover?

PAPAGENA

When he can his creed forget.

PAPAGENO

I believe I know who *he* is.

PAPAGENA

Yes, I know you think you know.

PAPAGENO

Do you *think* you know who *she* is?

PAPAGENA

No, I *know* I know her.

PAPAGENO

O!

Is she pretty?

PAPAGENA

Why deny it?

PAPAGENO

Is she young?

PAPAGENA

As young as you.

80

PAPAGENO
Is he old?

PAPAGENA
As old as I, it seems.

PAPAGENO
I know him?

PAPAGENA
Yes, you do.

PAPAGENO
Now I'm certain. You need say no more. I know your love
must be . . .

2ND PRIEST
[*off-stage*]
Papageno! Papageno!

PAPAGENA
You are right.

PAPAGENO
It's he, it's he!

[*Enter* 2ND PRIEST]
Well, dear guardian and guide, you are the person that we
need.
Come, relax, there's love inside you if you can forget your
creed.
I know whom you love.

2ND PRIEST
Whom *I* love?

PAPAGENO
You, but you don't
know it yet.
You love *her*.

2ND PRIEST
          She is not *my* love. *You* love her.

PAPAGENO
                                        Come, come,

my pet.

2ND PRIEST
She loves *you*.

PAPAGENO
          You're very stupid. She loves *you*.

2ND PRIEST
                                        You've lost

your mind.

PAPAGENO
You're no person to play Cupid.

2ND PRIEST
                              Maybe not. I am not blind.
[*They turn their backs on each other.*]

PAPAGENA
I love *him*. I don't love *you*.

PAPAGENO
                    You see.

2ND PRIEST
                         You see.

PAPAGENA
                              And *he* loves *me*.

PAPAGENO
I don't love you.

2ND PRIEST
          Don't you?

PAPAGENA

Do you? I love *you.*

PAPAGENO

You see.

2ND PRIEST

You
see.

PAPAGENO

I know whom I love.

2ND PRIEST

You think so?

PAPAGENO

And whom I love *not.*

2ND PRIEST

Re-
call. . . .

PAPAGENO

Really, sir, I think you drink so much you cannot see at all.

2ND PRIEST

I drink!

PAPAGENO

You!

2ND PRIEST

And you!

PAPAGENO

Well, I know *how* and still know truth
from lies.

Nose and ear and hand and eye know how to make a person
  wise.
That's what *I* believe the most.

2ND PRIEST

The creed you must forget.
  Recall
This: the louder that you boast, the harder then shall be your
  fall.
Senses oft deceive . . .

PAPAGENO

One minute! Talk of boasting, old im-
  biber!
You vowed *me* a lovely linnet, went so far as to describe her;
Now you *dare* suppose—in *vain*—a *new* love for me, old
  supposer!
If there *is* a Papagena, stop your boasting and disclose her
Now! Delay no more, old feigner!

2ND PRIEST
[*leading* PAPAGENA *to him*]

Here!

PAPAGENO

Not *her*!

PRIEST
[*removing* PAPAGENA's *disguise*]

Look well

and love her!

PAPAGENA
Papageno!

PAPAGENO
>Papagena!

2ND PRIEST
>Back! You are not worthy of her!
[PRIEST *whisks* PAPAGENA *away.*]

PAPAGENO
Woe is me! I cannot bear it. Those three witches warned me. Where
Has she gone? O do I merit such a fate for taking care?
Is it *fair?* It isn't fair. It *isn't* fair. It isn't *fair!*

Scene IV

[Same as Scene II. Moonlight.]

SPIRITS
Soon dawn on earth and ocean breaking
    Will drive all shadows far away,
And men from their illusions waking
    Salute with grateful joy the candid day.
Come, holy ray, our darkness brighten
    And with thy wisdom our foolish hearts enlighten,
That truth may be revealed to all
    And every vain idol fall.

1ST SPIRIT
But O, Pamina may not hearken.

2ND *and* 3RD SPIRITS
Though light is near . . .

1ST SPIRIT
                    Her senses darken.

SPIRITS
While all await the joyous morrow,
She grieves her yesterday of sorrow
With disillusionment and fear.
O that Tamino could be here!

She comes, her stainless aspect wild.
We must protect the noble child.
    [*Enter* PAMINA, *holding the dagger before her.*]

    PAMINA
You are my love, my love's reward,
My mother's sorrow, my future lord.

    SPIRITS
Her words are dark with sad intent.
We dare not understand their bent.

    PAMINA
My life, my traitor, hold with me—
O heart of steel,
The fatal rites are soon to be;
My heart shall wed eternity.

    SPIRITS
Furies of the night pursue her;
Desperation will undo her.
Fair Pamina, stay your hand!

    PAMINA
Do not hold me! Love's command
To this heart where love was stronger
Is that it shall beat no longer;
By this hand will heart comply.

    SPIRITS
Damned all self-destroyers die!

    PAMINA
Life you gave and in my keeping
Gave this charm to still my weeping,

O my mother. Through darkness she calls
And her curse upon me falls!

SPIRITS

Hear us! Die not in despair!

PAMINA

Take, for nought remains to tell,
Faithless lover, my farewell.
Let Pamina seek release,
By this steel I find my peace.

SPIRITS

[*taking the dagger from her*]
Dear unfortunate, forbear!
With one death would come a second:
From your grave would love have beckoned
And have slain Tamino there!

PAMINA

Love? But if he loved me would he
Turn away from me or could he
By his silence, love deny?
Or desert me? Tell me why?

SPIRITS

We may give no explanation.
You shall meet, and revelation
At the sight of him ensue.
Know that he, at love's command,
Faces death to win your hand.
Come with us and find him true!

PAMINA

Faithful love, I come to you!

PAMINA *and* SPIRITS
When lovers to their lover tender
The lives that they may not surrender,
Then love their safety will provide,
The gods their footsteps guard and guide.
    [*Exeunt.*]

Scene V

[Before the Caves of Fire and Water, the entrances to which are guarded by two men in armor.]

C H O R A L E

ARMED MEN

Now shall the pilgrim tread a valley dark and dire,
Face death by air and water, earth and fire.
Who shall this dreadful passage to the end endure,
He his salvation shall thereby secure,
In mansions of the Light forever dwell;
Isis her mysteries to him shall fully tell.

———————

TAMINO

No fear of death shall daunt or bate me
The gates of hell already wait me;
I hear their dreadful hinges groan
My feet must dare the path alone.

PAMINA
[off-stage]
Tamino, stay! I come with you.

TAMINO
Do I hear Pamina calling?

ARMED MEN
You hear, you hear Pamina calling.

TAMINO *and* ARMED MEN
The gods permit that she come too:
Now nothing can our (your) lives divide
Though Fate a mutual death decide.

TAMINO
My vow? Am I released from silence?

ARMED MEN
Henceforth you are released from silence.

TAMINO *and* ARMED MEN
What joy a common fate to share,
Thus hand in hand the way to dare!
A love that death for love defies
Is matchless, dear in Heaven's eyes.

PAMINA
[*entering*]
Forever mine, in life, in death.

TAMINO
Forever mine, in life, in death.

With threatening sad faces
Grim spectres beckon me.

PAMINA
In savage and in dismal places
Beside you I shall be.
No harm can us betide
For love shall be our guide
And love can make the desert bloom,

Can turn to spring the winter's gloom.
Your flute shall also play its part
Defending us by magic art.
With spell and runes of secret power
'Twas fashioned in a moonless hour,
Was carved from immemorial oak
To flash of lightning, thunderstroke.
So take the magic flute and play,
To make of night a cheerful day.

      TAMINO, PAMINA *and* ARMED MEN
We (they) wander through the horrid shade,
Of death and darkness unafraid.

    [TAMINO, *playing the flute, leads* PAMINA *through the
      Cave of Fire.*]

      TAMINO *and* PAMINA
    [*emerging*]
Sweet notes that with your soft compulsion
    Retired the elemental flame,
Rebuke the watery convulsion,
    The flood in all its fury tame.

    [*They enter the Cave of Water.*]

Scene **V I**

*[*TAMINO *and* PAMINA *emerge before the Temple, which is brightly lit.]*

TAMINO *and* PAMINA
O dazzling splendor of the light!
O world, so lovely, green and bright!

CHORUS
'Tis done, 'tis done, your Quest is done.
The crown of Wisdom you have won.
Come to the temple, happy pair,
Advance. Advance.
Gods and men your triumph share.

Scene VII

[*Same as Scene IV—Night. Enter* PAPAGENO *with a noose.*]

PAPAGENO

Papagena! Papagena! Come be near me!
Linnet! Pippit! Can you hear me?
No answer. Ah! All is predestined:
Can my unlucky stars be questioned?
Should I have shown bravery? It's not for me:
Lovebirds can no more eagles be
Than a she can be a he.

I am not certain she was real.
The Order may have played a trick.
Yet I am certain how I feel:
I am in love; and I am sick.
Papagena, lovely linnet!
Papagena, pretty pippit!
O that wine had something in it!
What a fool I was to sip it,
For it made me love and I
Am unloved and want to die.
       [*Pointing to a tree*]

I shall hang here like a letter,
For my body will say better
Than my mind could ever spell:
O you wicked world, farewell!
To the forceful and the forceless
You are equally remorseless.
I am sorry I was born.
Tell the pretty girls to mourn.

Will not one of them take pity?
Even if she's not so pretty
She could win me from my woe:
Is it yes? Or is it no?

I hear nothing, no replying.
Was it worth my trying?
No one cares that I am dying.

Like a bird I must through air
Fly the grounds of my despair;
So, you broken-hearted dove,
Be a man and die for love.

Come, my rescuer, to me.
I'm waiting here. Come. I'll be
Waiting till . . . I . . . count . . . to . . . three.
One. Two. Three.
No reply—O futile plea!—
No reply to constancy.

Love can find no place to dwell;
So you wicked world, farewell.
O you wicked world, farewell.

SPIRITS
[*appearing suddenly*]
Forbear, forbear, O Papageno! If you choose
To throw away your life now, you will lose
The only life you'll ever have to use.

PAPAGENO
You boyish Spirits are well-spoken,
But you have no hearts to be broken.
If I were disembodied too
I'd miss nobody as I do.

SPIRITS
Pick up your chimes and set them ringing
To bring your lovely linnet winging.

PAPAGENO
Now how could I have thought of swinging?
Forgotten chimes, you start me singing!
Ring out, and with your ting-a-linging
Remind my absent sweetheart of
Her Papageno and her love.

Tingle, chimes, a summons, bring my dear to me.
Tingle, chimes, a summons! Bring her here to me.
Bring her back, my only love, the love for me.

SPIRITS
[*ushering in* PAPAGENA]
Now, Papageno, turn and see!

96

[*Exeunt* SPIRITS.]

PAPAGENO

Pa-pa-pa-pa-papagena!

PAPAGENA

Pa-pa-pa-pa-papageno!

PAPAGENO

Are you mine to love completely?

PAPAGENA

Yours forever, yours completely!

PAPAGENO

Will you be my loving linnet?

PAPAGENA

I shall be your faithful pippit!

PAPAGENO *and* PAPAGENA

Heaven will augment our joys,
Will approve our love by sending
To our nest a dear, unending
Lovely brood of girls and boys,
An unending brood of girls and boys.

PAPAGENO

First, first a little Papageno.

PAPAGENA

Then, then a little Papagena.

PAPAGENO

Then, then another Papageno.

PAPAGENA

Then, then another Papagena.

PAPAGENO *and* PAPAGENA

What better blessings to have more of?

A score of
Papagenos,
Papagenas,
To be the comforts of our life,
To make us truly man and wife.

Scene VIII

[*A rocky place. Night.* ASTRAFIAMMANTE *and her* LADIES *enter, led by* MONOSTATOS.]

MONOSTATOS
We must be quiet, quiet, quiet
If we are not to be espied.

ASTRAFIAMMANTE *and* LADIES
We must be quiet near the temple
And in familiar darkness hide.

MONOSTATOS
Your Highness, shall I wed Pamina?
You swore I should, were we allied.

ASTRAFIAMMANTE
You had our word, impassioned ally,
We swore our child should be your bride:
The Queen will by her oath abide.

3RD LADY
The Queen will keep her promise,
Will by her oath abide.

1ST *and* 2ND LADIES
The Queen of Night will by her oath abide.

MONOSTATOS
But what is quickening the darkness?

What can that ruthless roaring be?

ASTRAFIAMMANTE *and* LADIES
O dreadful seems the pregnant darkness,
Each lawless element set free.

MONOSTATOS
In rites convening is the Order.

ALL
Upon their rites shall rain disorder,
Upon their gaudy day descend
A moonless midnight with no end.

MONOSTATOS *and* LADIES
Astrafiammante, Queen of Night!
May we achieve our vengeance tonight!
[*Thunder and lightning.*]

ALL
What blinds us with lightning! What binds us with fright?
We sink to the chaos of infinite night!
[*They sink into the ground.*]

Scene I X

SARASTRO

The sun's golden glory has conquered the night:
Original Darkness gives way to the Light.
>[SARASTRO *takes off his crown and places it on* TAMINO'S
>*head.*]

CHORUS

Glory to the Holy Ones,
Everlasting glory,
Our guardians and our guides! Amen!
Isis and Osiris! Amen!
>[SARASTRO *leads* TAMINO *and* PAMINA *up to two thrones.*]

Unfurl your brave banners, let trumpets be blown,
For Wisdom and Beauty are mounting the throne.
>[PAPAGENO *and* PAPAGENA *appear from behind the
>thrones and sit at their feet.*]

Unfurl your brave banners, let trumpets be blown,
For Wisdom and Beauty have mounted the throne.

[*Curtain*]

Postscript

[ASTRAFIAMMANTE *to the Translators.*]

"*For Wisdom and Beauty have mounted the throne*"
May be your parting words, but the last is Our own:
It is We who dismiss, as you ought to have known.

In Act Two, We observed, you saw fit to contrive
A later appearance for Us and deprive
Our rage of its dialogue: We shall survive

To laugh, unimpressed, at your liberal correction
Of conservative views about women's subjection;
Male vanity's always been Our best protection.

You may think, if you will, your New Order excuses
Putting Us in Our place, but it merely amuses:
Little men, have you any idea who your Muse is?

As for Wisdom and Beauty in heart-warming bliss,
Upon whom do they call every time that they kiss
But the blood-curdling Queen of the Kingdom of Dis?

To that realm We descend when Our cue has been sounded
(Obedient to music) and there rule unbounded
Where your loves are enforced and your fantasies founded.

Schikaneder and Giesecke clung to the hope a
Stage trap-door would bury this dark interloper,
But We'll never lack friends back in Mittel-Europa.

We were Goethe's Die Mütter, an understage chorus,
Then for Wagner We half-rose as Erda, now for Us
Freud adds a blunt synonym to the thesaurus.

So english, remodel Our lines as you please,
Unscramble the drama and jumble the keys:
That will serve for the rest of the cast—and your fees.

Let the Press laud your language as sharper and purer
Than the German can boast: when We strike in Our furor,
You won't hear a word in Our high tessitura.

And it won't be with diction, industrialized dull sirs,
Who with graph, daylight-saving and stop-watch repulse Us,
That We strike, but with hangover, sinus and ulcers.

Though translated to Hell, We still govern, a light
That wanes but to wax; whether shrouded or bright,
We are always Queen Astrafiammante:—Good night!

Notes

* An asterisk following a line in the text indicates that a slight musical change is required in the score.

ª The German is written in regular octosyllabics.

> Der Vögelfänger bin ich ja,
> Stets lustig heisa hop-sa-sa!
> Ich Vögelfänger bin bekannt
> Bei alt und jung im ganzen Land, etc.

In this song and in several places throughout the text, we have taken the liberty of writing more syllables than exist in the original when our ears so advised. The English language has fewer syllables than the German which sound well when spread over more than one note. If it be asked: "Is the effect the same?" the answer, of course, is "No. The English sounds more staccato than the German." We believe, however, that *The Magic Flute* should sound more staccato than *Die Zauberflöte*.

*

ᵇ The German lyric is written in iambic rhythm, i.e., in 4/4 time. This Mozart has set to a tune in 6/8, so that certain syllables have to be spread over two notes, linked by a slur, thus:

1 2 1   2 1 2 1 1 1
Bei Männern, welche Liebe fühlen,
1   2   1 2 1 2 1 1
Fehlt auch ein gutes Herze nicht.
1 2 1   2 1 2 1 1 1
Die süssen Triebe mitzufühlen
1 1 1   2 1 2 1   1
Ist dann der Weiber erste Pflicht.

In translating this, we found that the English language cried out for
an anapestic rhythm, similar to that of the notes. If the original
relation of syllables to notes is not an accident of the German
prosody but a profound musical idea, then, of course, we are wrong,
so he who is pedantic, let him be pedantic still and sing instead:

When Love his dart has deep implanted,
The Hero's heart grows kind and tame,
And by his passion soon enchanted,
The nymph receives the impetuous flame.
    In all our days, etc.

For Love is Lord throughout all nature
And all to his command must yield;
He comforts every living creature,
The birds in air, the beasts of the field.
    The highest goal, etc.

*

c In translating recitative, as contrasted with arias or ensembles, the actual sense and dramatic intensity of what is said must take precedence over the form. This particular passage of recitative is rhymed in the German, e.g.:

> Die Weisheits lehre dieser Knaben
> Sei ewig im mir ins Herz gegraben.
> Wo bin ich nun? Was wird mit mir?
> Ist dies der Sitz der Götter hier?

Naturally, it is technically possible to copy this, but the result must almost inevitably be operese, not English, since the feminine rhymes so common in German are rare in our own tongue and the majority of those which do exist are comic.

Take, for instance, the couplet

> Riss nicht der Rauber ohn Erbarmen
> Pamina aus der Mutter Armen.

One can fiddle about with this in such a way that the second line ends on a rhymable feminine ending like *mother,* but all dramatic force will be lost unless this line is rendered literally, which means a masculine ending. In lieu of rhymes, we have tried to link the questions and answers of this recitative by repeating key words, a device common in the stichomythia of Greek tragedy. Thus, to Tamino's question

> Did he not steal, did he not ravish
> Pamina from her mother's arms?

the priest replies

> He took her from her mother's arms.

A similar difficulty arises with Tamino's anguished demand to the invisible spirits

> Lebt sich Pamina noch?

Nothing will do here but the direct and simple

> Is Pamina still alive?

Any exact prosodic equivalents of the German like *O does Pamina live?* or *Lives then Pamina still?* are stylistically and emotionally impossible. To preserve the essentials of the musical phrase, a strong accent must be thrown upon the first syllable, thus:

> Is Pāmĭnā stĭll ălīve?

*

[d] The German word *geschwinde* when spoken ends in a trochee, but as set here is turned into a spondee. The trouble about any appropriate English equivalent like *hurry* is that it cannot be sung as a spondee without sounding distorted. Seeing that, a page earlier, Mozart sets to the same musical phrase a line with a masculine ending

> sonst erwischen sie uns noch

we believe that he would have no profound objection to a change.

*

e Mein Kind, was werden wir nun sprechen?
Die Wahrheit, die Wahrheit! war sie auch Verbrechen.

Alas, what can a translator do with this, one of the most beautiful moments in the opera? There is nothing Pamina can possibly say in English but *The Truth* and that is a syllable short. *Be truthful* and *The whole Truth* are flat. One cannot spread *Truth* over two notes and sing *troo-hooth* without sounding funny. But whatever word one adds detracts from the intensity of the original.

*

f Es lebe Sarastro, der gottliche Weise!
Er lohnet, er strafet in ähnlichen Kreise.

Again, the old problem of the feminine ending. If they so wish, the fussy may sing:

Give praise to Sarastro; his word shall perséver,
For just are his dealings, enduring forever.

*

g See page 13, lines 11-13.

*

h See page 31, lines 8-10.

*

108

¹In the German dialogue, the Queen appears alone and speaks herself. We have introduced her three ladies to speak on her behalf for two reasons. It is more seemly that a semi-divine character like the Queen never descend from the heights of song to mortal speech, and the speaking voice of a coloratura soprano is rarely majestic.

*

ʲ*Light and Truth.* The German is set thus:

Wurdi-ig sein.

The English syllables, it seems to us, should be differently distributed:

Li-ight and Truth.